WHALES SET II

FIN WHALES

Kristin Petrie
ABDO Publishing Company

visit us at
www.abdopub.com

Published by ABDO Publishing Company, 4940 Viking Drive, Edina, Minnesota 55435.
Copyright © 2006 by Abdo Consulting Group, Inc. International copyrights reserved in all countries. No part of this book may be reproduced in any form without written permission from the publisher. The Checkerboard Library™ is a trademark and logo of ABDO Publishing Company.

Printed in the United States.

Cover Photo: © Mark Jones / SeaPics.com
Interior Photos: © Carlos Navarro / SeaPics.com p. 15; Corel pp. 8, 17; © Kevin Schafer / SeaPics.com p. 19; © Lori Mazzuca / SeaPics.com p. 5; © Mark Ruth / SeaPics.com p. 10; © Michael S. Nolan / SeaPics.com pp. 7, 11, 12, 21; Peter Arnold p. 13; Uko Gorter p. 6

Series Coordinator: Stephanie Hedlund
Editors: Stephanie Hedlund, Megan Murphy
Art Direction & Maps: Neil Klinepier

Library of Congress Cataloging-in-Publication Data

Petrie, Kristin, 1970-
    Fin whales / Kristin Petrie.
        p. cm. -- (Whales. Set II)
    ISBN 1-59679-309-0
    1. Finback whale--Juvenile literature. I. Title.

QL737.C424P38 2005
599.5'24--dc22
                                                                    2005046948

CONTENTS

FIN WHALES AND FAMILY

Mammals are animals that breathe air, have live young, and nurse their young. Mammals come in all shapes and sizes. Do you know what the second-largest mammal in the world is?

The fin whale is second in size only to the blue whale. The fin whale weighs 50 to 70 tons (45 to 65 t). Both of these enormous mammals are **rorqual baleen** whales. They are able to grow so large because the waters they live in support their weight.

The fin whale is also known as the "greyhound of the oceans." That is because it is fast like a greyhound dog, even though it is a massive animal. The fin whale can swim up to 23 miles per hour (37 km/h)!

The scientific name for the fin whale is *Balaenoptera physalus*. It is part of the Balaenopteridae family of **baleen** whales. There are eight species in this family.

The name Balaenoptera *means "winged whale."* Physalus *means "bellows," which may refer to the fin whale's expanding mouth or its blow.*

Shape, Size, and Color

The fin whale is long and sleek. Its huge head is up to one-quarter of its whole body. This enormous head is flat and V-shaped.

The fin whale has 50 to 100 throat grooves that run from its mouth to its belly. These grooves allow its mouth to expand for feeding. This expanding mouth is what makes it a **rorqual** whale.

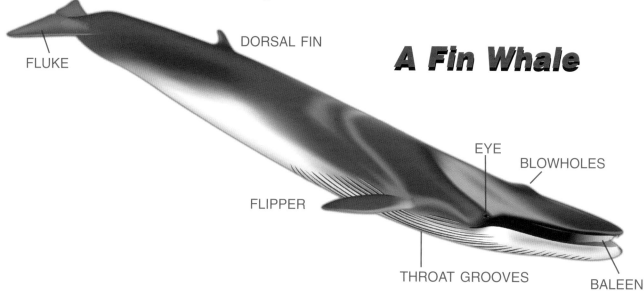

DORSAL FIN

FLUKE

A Fin Whale

EYE

BLOWHOLES

FLIPPER

THROAT GROOVES

BALEEN

Like other **baleen** whales, the fin whale has two blowholes. Behind the blowholes is a curved **dorsal** fin. A ridge behind the dorsal fin gives the fin whale another nickname, the razorback.

Small, rounded flippers stick out from the whale's sides. The flukes, or tail fins, have pointed tips and a notched center.

Fin whales don't usually raise their flukes when diving. So, this is a rare sight!

Fin whales are huge. Fully grown fin whales can be 88 feet (27 m) long. Like most **cetaceans**, females are larger than males.

One **trait** makes this whale stand out from the rest. It looks like it is tie-dyed! This whale's back, sides, and tail are gray or black. Its belly and the right side of the lower jaw are white. But, the left side of the jaw is gray. Lighter streaks of color loop from head to tail.

WHERE THEY LIVE

Fin whales are found in all of the world's oceans. And, they are the only **rorqual** whale to venture into the Mediterranean Sea.

Fin whales like cold water better than warm water. Some fin whales **migrate** between cold feeding areas and warm mating areas. They are usually found outside the **continental slope**.

Fin whales can often be seen in the same places throughout the year.

But sometimes, they are seen close to the shore if the water is more than 650 feet (200 m) deep.

There are several groups of fin whales. Some groups are in the northern **hemisphere**.

Others are in the southern **hemisphere**. Because the
seasons of these hemispheres are opposite, the whales
migrate toward the equator at different times. So, fin
whales can be seen near the equator year-round.

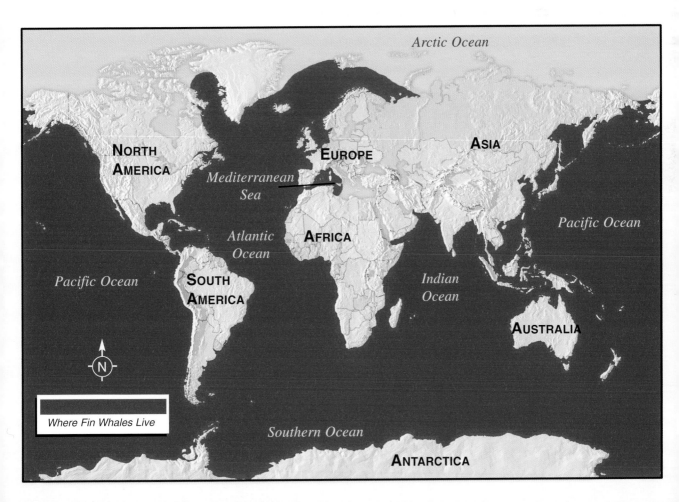

Arctic Ocean

NORTH
AMERICA

EUROPE

ASIA

Mediterranean
Sea

Pacific Ocean

Atlantic
Ocean

AFRICA

Pacific Ocean

SOUTH
AMERICA

Indian
Ocean

AUSTRALIA

N

Where Fin Whales Live

Southern Ocean

ANTARCTICA

SENSES

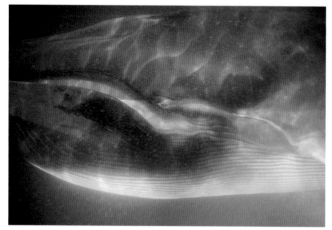

All whales have eyes with special features that allow them to see underwater. One of these features is a thicker outer covering on the lens.

The fin whale's **habitat** is huge! To keep from getting lost, fin whales must use their senses. Like most **cetaceans**, their most useful sense is hearing.

Whales and other marine life use sounds to communicate. They also use sounds to find mates and food. Some turn those sounds into information. This is called echolocation.

Most **baleen** whales don't use echolocation. But, fin whales have shown that they may use some form of the sense. They may use it to find and herd food.

With echolocation, whales make pictures in their minds from sounds. They produce clicks that travel through the water. Echoes bounce off an object and return. This echoed noise may tell the whale its location. Or, it may warn of danger!

Sounds can travel great distances in water. So, cetaceans use clicks, moans, and whistles to talk to each other.

DEFENSE

The speedy fin whale doesn't have many **predators**. Killer whales may be its only natural enemy. In the past, even whalers couldn't catch the speedy mammals.

However, the invention of the harpoon gun made the fin whale easier to hunt. Over the years, thousands were killed. Their numbers dropped quickly.

Fin whales may have parasites, which are creatures that live on other animals. Whales will jump out of the water, or breach, to get rid of them.

In 1966, fin whales became protected by the International Whaling Commission. Now, whaling is closely regulated. Natives in Greenland are allowed to hunt 19 whales per year.

They are only allowed to kill the amount needed to feed and maintain certain cultures.

Scientists believe there are about 70,000 fin whales left at this time. Like many **baleen** whales, they are considered **vulnerable** to extinction.

At one time, there may have been about 470,000 fin whales. But these whales are large, and they provide much meat, oil, and baleen. So, they were a main whaling target for many years.

FOOD

With that huge mouth, you would think the fin whale must eat big stuff. But surprisingly, one of the largest animals feasts on some of the smallest sea life.

Fin whales feed mainly on **plankton** and euphausiids, which are small creatures called krill. In the summer, fin whales eat up to 2,000 pounds (900 kg) of krill a day! They also enjoy schooling fish.

Eating that many tiny animals is a big job. So, the fin whale has an expanding throat. The fin whale must take in huge amounts of water to get enough tiny food. Every drop of this water is filtered by the fin whale's teeth. These "teeth" are really called **baleen**.

Baleen are comblike plates that hang from the whale's upper jaw. The fin whale's baleen plates are up to 30 inches (75 cm) long and 12 inches (30 cm) wide. Fin whales have up to 800 baleen plates!

Fin whales eat by lunge feeding. To do this, they open their mouths and rush to the surface of the water.

The inside of a **baleen** plate has hairy edges. All kinds of food, from **plankton** to **crustaceans**, get caught in it. When the whale closes its mouth, water is pushed out. The food is swallowed, however.

BABIES

Fin whales eat to have energy to mate and reproduce. Fin whales are ready to mate when they are six to ten years old. Most fin whales **migrate** to warm mating waters.

A fin whale is **pregnant** for 12 months. A female needs this time to produce a large baby, called a calf. Newborn calves may be up to 20 feet (6 m) long. They weigh about 4,000 pounds (1,800 kg).

Fin whales reproduce about every three to four years. The mother whale nurses her young with milk. The young whale is **weaned** when it has grown to about 30 to 40 feet (9 to 12 m) in length. Fin whales live approximately 80 years.

Some fin whales have been recorded at 114 years old!

BEHAVIORS

Fin whales usually keep to themselves. If they get lonely, they will hang out with a few other whales in a pod. Sometimes, a larger number of fin whales will get together. During long **migrations**, a pod with 50 to 300 members may swim together!

Fin whales can be identified at sea in several ways. Their **blow** is shaped like an upside-down cone. Five to eight blows appear from the water's surface before a long dive. Fin whales can dive up to 1,800 feet (550 m) deep for three to ten minutes.

The fin whale's coloring may be its most unusual feature. Scientists are not sure of the reason for this odd coloring. But, the whale is often seen feeding with the white side facing down.

Opposite page: *A fin whale surfaces with its blowholes showing first. This sets it apart from both sei and Bryde's whales, whose blowholes and dorsal fins surface at the same time.*

Fin Whale Facts

Scientific Name: *Balaenoptera physalus*

Common Name: Fin Whale

Other Names: Finback, Finner, Common Rorqual, Razorback, Herring Whale

Average Size:
Length - 88 feet (27 m)
Weight - 50 to 70 tons (45 to 65 t)

Where They Are Found: In all of the world's oceans and the Mediterranean Sea

This view of the fin whale shows its unique coloring. When looking straight on, the left side of the jaw is white but the right side is gray. This coloring is also found on the whale's baleen!

GLOSSARY

baleen - of or relating to the tough, hornlike material that hangs from the upper jaw of certain whales. Baleen is used to filter food.

blow - a mix of air and water droplets that are released when a marine mammal breathes.

Cetacea - an order of mammal, such as the whale, that lives in the water like fish. Members of this order are called cetaceans.

continental slope - the steep slope that drops from a continent to the ocean floor.

crustacean (kruhs-TAY-shuhn) - any of a group of animals with hard shells that live mostly in water. Crabs, lobsters, and shrimps are all crustaceans.

dorsal - located near or on the back, especially of an animal.

habitat - a place where a living thing is naturally found.

hemisphere - one half of Earth.

migrate - to move from one place to another, often to find food.

plankton - small animals and plants that float in a body of water.

predator - an animal that kills and eats other animals.

pregnant - having one or more babies growing within the body.

rorqual - any baleen whale with grooves that allow its throat to expand for feeding.

trait - a quality that distinguishes one person or group from another.

vulnerable - open to being hurt or attacked.

wean - to accustom an animal to eat food other than its mother's milk.

WEB SITES

To learn more about fin whales, visit ABDO Publishing Company on the World Wide Web at **www.abdopub.com**. Web sites about these whales are featured on our Book Links page. These links are routinely monitored and updated to provide the most current information available.

INDEX

A

Arctic Ocean 8
Atlantic Ocean 8

B

Balaenopteridae 5
baleen plates 14, 15
baleen whales 4, 5, 7, 10, 13
blowholes 7
blows 18
blue whale 4
body 6, 7

C

calves 16
cetaceans 7, 10
color 7, 18

D

defense 11, 12
diving 18
dorsal fin 7

E

echolocation 10, 11

F

flippers 7
food 6, 8, 10, 14, 15, 16, 18

H

head 6, 7

I

Indian Ocean 8
International Whaling Commission 12

K

killer whales 12

L

life span 16

M

mammals 4, 12
Mediterranean Sea 8
migration 8, 9, 16, 18

P

Pacific Ocean 8
pods 18
population 12, 13
predators 12

R

reproduction 8, 10, 16
rorqual whales 4, 6, 8

S

senses 10, 11
size 4, 6, 7, 14, 16
sounds 10, 11
speed 4, 12

T

tail 7
throat grooves 6, 14

W

whaling 12, 13

24